Behind Every
Good Man

Behind Every Good Man

HELPING YOUR HUSBAND TAKE THE SPIRITUAL LEAD AT HOME

JOHN BYTHEWAY

DESERET
BOOK
SALT LAKE CITY, UTAH

Library of Congress Cataloging-in-Publication Data

Bytheway, John, 1962–
   Behind every good man : helping your husband take the spiritual lead at home / John Bytheway.
        p.   cm.
   Includes bibliographical references and index.
   ISBN 978-1-60641-072-1 (paperbound)
   1. Family—Religious aspects—Church of Jesus Christ of Latter-day Saints.   2. Sex role—Religious aspects—Church of Jesus Christ of Latter-day Saints.   I. Title.
   BX8643.F3B97 2009
   248.8'44—dc22   2008053668

Printed in the United States of America
Worzalla Publishing Co., Stevens Point, WI

10   9   8   7   6   5   4   3   2   1

Contents

Acknowledgments

I am indebted to my wife, Kimberly, and to my sisters-in-law, Jennifer Dustin, Natalie Loveridge, Tiffany Johnson, and Amy Hendrickson, who read the initial draft of this book and made helpful and insightful suggestions. I am also indebted to Dr. John L. Lund, who allowed me to quote him extensively in this book.

I am grateful to Sheri Dew and Laurel Christensen, who have given me the opportunity to participate in numerous *Time Out for Women* events, where I've been privileged to meet and mingle with many wonderful women and learn of their concerns.

Special thanks to Emily Watts for her editorial skills, Shauna Gibby for her design, Rachael Ward for the typesetting, and Chris Schoebinger for his constant encouragement and guidance.

We Were Stumped

A few years ago, at a *Time Out for Women* event in Cincinnati, I sat with a few of the faculty eager to begin a Q & A session. Near the end of our lighthearted exchange with the attendees, one woman raised her hand and said, "How can we get our husbands to take the lead on things like family home evening and scripture study?"

I was relieved there was a marriage counselor sitting beside me, so I just looked to my right and waited. But he didn't answer right away. We were stumped. At least I was. The marriage counselor was in a tough spot too. How do you answer a question like that in two minutes? You can't, and he couldn't—at least not adequately. When the event was over, I felt some regret that we never really answered her question.

I've been haunted by the memory of that Q & A ever since. I am one of those who likes to think the gospel has the best answer to *every* problem. I still believe that. And I still have the picture in my head of this woman standing on her feet and asking the question—and of seeing many other women nod their heads as she asked. She used the pronouns "how can *we* get *our* husbands" as if she were speaking for more than just herself, and perhaps she was.

A few months of pondering over that woman's question brought me to conclude that what she was really asking was this: How do I get a change of heart—*for someone else?*

Similar questions might be: How can I help

*How many psychologists does it
take to change a lightbulb?*

One.

*But the lightbulb
has to want to change.*

someone forgive a family member for a past offense? How can I get my son to desire to serve a mission, or my daughter to realize she needs to break up with the boy she's dating? Or a husband might want to ask, how can I get my wife to find more contentment in motherhood? So this is a much broader question than just hoping to get someone to exhibit a certain behavior. This is a plea to get someone else to grow and change and be spiritually transformed.

As I travel around participating in youth conferences, quite frequently a young person will hand me an e-mail address and say, "Would you please write to my friend? They're not coming to seminary anymore," or, "They're inactive; would you please write them and fix that?" (or words to that effect). On those occasions, I'm left feeling inadequate and helpless. The scriptures are very clear about what *I* must do to be spiritually transformed, but how do I bring about that transformation in someone else?

When you can adequately answer that question, please FedEx your double-spaced manuscript to Deseret Book for immediate publication.

And the Answer Is . . .

꧁꧂

Sorry, there's no easy answer. Although it may be a righteous desire to want someone else to live up to his or her potential more fully, you can't order a change of heart for another person. If it were possible to change hearts by remote control, the story of Laman and Lemuel, the story of Alma the Younger, and the stories of countless other children or spouses of faithful Saints would be a lot different.

Certainly we can pray and plead with the Lord

for help in behalf of others, and ask him to intervene, but even then, as the hymn reminds us:

> *Know this, that ev'ry soul is free*
> *To choose his life and what he'll be;*
> *For this eternal truth is giv'n:*
> *That God will force no man to heav'n.*[1]

Even Jesus, with his incomparable gifts of loving and serving and teaching, couldn't force a change of heart on the scribes and Pharisees (at least not without violating agency, which he simply wouldn't do). That being said, however, there are many things that might *help*. So take heart!

We're given a list of words and phrases in Doctrine and Covenants 121 that express how we should deal with others without using coercion: *persuasion, long-suffering, gentleness, meekness, love unfeigned,* and *kindness* (see D&C 121:41–42). It will be vital to keep these terms in mind as we continue our discussion.

We have not succeeded in answering your problem. The answers we have found have only raised more questions. In some ways we feel we are as confused as ever. But we feel that we are confused on a higher level, and about more important things.

So the answer to the question the sister asked in Ohio would begin like this:

1. There are no easy answers.

2. However, there are a number of things that might help.

3. Even if the ideas that follow *don't* help with this specific problem, I have no doubt that they will bless your marriage in other ways.

Why Do People Change?

Nearly twenty years ago, my oldest brother had a "change of kidney." He got my left one. It required a couple of surgeons, anesthesiologists, half a dozen nurses, prayer, priesthood, fasting, and considerable postoperative care, but it worked, and we are eternally grateful.

When it comes to a change of heart, however, there's only one Being who can make that happen. We must rely on God. From a gospel perspective, the Holy Ghost is the one who changes people. Alma taught, "Behold, *he* changed their

"No one can change a person who is unwilling to change. Not even fear of death by cancer will stop the smoker who is unwilling to change. People don't change people. People change themselves or are changed by the Holy Ghost."

—Dr. John L. Lund[2]

hearts; yea, he awakened them out of a deep sleep, and they awoke unto God" (Alma 5:7; emphasis added). Alma the Younger was visited by an angel (see Mosiah 27), Paul was transformed by a vision on the road to Damascus (see Acts 9), David asked the Lord to create in him a clean heart (see Psalm 51:10). I suppose I could reference a dozen more verses, but I think we all know intuitively that God is the only one who changes hearts.

This gives us something to work with, doesn't it! We know that we must get God involved. We know that we must have the Spirit of the Lord present in our homes and in our marriages.

The Spirit Is Welcome Here

We often hear phrases in the Church that emphasize the importance of the Spirit in our lives: "Teach by the Spirit," "Listen with the Spirit," "Don't offend the Spirit," and so on.

Well, here's another one: "Invite the Spirit into your marriage." I realize that's kind of a general statement, and I suspect that when we hear similar advice, we think of things we can *do*—pray for each other, read scriptures, go to church together, choose wholesome entertainment. All of those are good ideas.

"That they may always have his Spirit to be with them. Amen."

—*D&C 20:77*

But there are a number of things we must *stop* doing if we really want the transforming power of the Spirit of the Lord present in our marriage. We must stop criticizing, we must stop resenting, we must stop holding onto grudges and refusing to forgive past offenses. Those things offend the Spirit, and without the Spirit, the kind of change we're hoping for may never occur. Having family scripture study and family prayer while holding onto resentments is like inviting the Spirit into our homes but refusing to kick the adversary out.

A number of years ago, the bishop in my ward taught a combined meeting of the high priests and elders. His lesson was so powerful, I took many notes. He was direct and bold, but he taught us with love. In a nutshell, this is what he said:

The single biggest problems in our ward are:
- The inability to forgive—particularly, a spouse's inability to get over something.
- Absence of expressions of love and support in our families. Many spouses or

family members haven't heard an honest, genuine "I love you" for years.

- Lack of priesthood leadership. Wives are becoming heads of homes; they convene family home evening and scripture study. Husbands and fathers have clearly been given this responsibility.

My bishop's third point, lack of priesthood leadership in the home, is the topic of this book. But isn't it interesting that the first two are directly related to maintaining the presence of the Spirit? It is my belief that these three are not only related but intertwined—and that we will never resolve one of them unless we also resolve the other two.

Criticism Doesn't
Bring Change

We know that the Spirit has the power to change people, and we also know something that doesn't. *Rarely is anyone criticized into change.* It just doesn't work. And criticism is offensive to the Spirit of the Lord, the very Spirit that is a vital ingredient to help our marriage grow.

Knowing what we know about marriage in the Lord's plan, it should be obvious to us that Satan wants us to dwell on the faults of our spouses. He loves it when we focus on their shortcomings and let our frustrations fester. Satan wants to see marriages struggle. He delights in our resentments and our contention. He longs to hear criticism. He wants pride. As the evil spirit, he doesn't want the Holy Spirit anywhere near our marriages, because the Holy Spirit brings growth and humility and change for the better.

When I'm tempted to think of things I wish my wife would do, I simply think of all the things *I* should be doing, and I'm suddenly very forgiving. The critical spirit leaves, a spirit of humility returns, and my focus turns more inward.

The fact is, we need each other. Satan knows this, so he tries to turn us into adversaries. In our popular culture, women criticize men, and men criticize women. Current philosophies teach that women don't need men, and men don't need women, and that we would all be more "liberated" without marriage. One writer even suggested that marriage is "slavery for women."

Have you noticed how men are portrayed in

"The objective of those who give criticism is to change the one being criticized. Often the critic is hopeful of a change of heart or an improved behavior. Criticism is extremely toxic to the human spirit. It is more likely to kill the desire for change than it is to inspire it."

—Dr. John L. Lund[3]

sitcoms these days? They are often depicted as lazy, insensitive, sports-addicted idiots. Sadly, these "gender wars" have real casualties. They degrade marriage. In fact, they degrade all of us, breaking up families and causing children to suffer as a result. This is exactly what Satan wants.

God, on the other hand, wants our marriages to succeed. He wants love and forgiveness and humility in our homes. In all my interactions with my wife and children, I have to remind myself that I am either serving God and his purposes or serving the devil and his. King Benjamin, while speaking to families who sat listening together in their tents, set up the contrast beautifully:

> And ye will not suffer your children that they go hungry, or naked; neither will ye suffer that they transgress the laws of God, and fight and quarrel one with another, and serve the devil, who is the master of sin, or who is the evil spirit which hath been spoken of by our fathers, he being an enemy to all righteousness.

> But ye will teach them to walk in the ways
> of truth and soberness; ye will teach them to
> love one another, and to serve one another.
> (Mosiah 4:14–15)

This isn't rocket science, nor is it deep theology. The idea of avoiding contention is just common sense. But unfortunately, indulging in criticism is common practice. One of the definitions of *insanity* is to continue to do the same thing while expecting a different result. Criticism doesn't work! "Constructive criticism" is an oxymoron. Elder H. Burke Peterson taught:

> I personally have a hard time with people who
> say they believe in constructive criticism. My
> experience does not lead me to believe there
> is such a thing. My point of view is that criticism has a connotation that does not come
> from above. I think it is important to note that
> *correction* is different from *criticism*. The Lord
> discussed correction in his revelation to the

Prophet Joseph Smith (see D&C 121:43). He emphasized that any corrections are to be per-formed when "moved upon by the Holy Ghost."[4]

I suspect that most of us, when we are tempted to criticize, are not being moved upon by the Holy Ghost, but are more often respond-ing to frustration from unmet expectations. Elder Peterson continued, "Criticism is more judgment-oriented than correction, and most of us do not have sufficient knowledge to be critical of others—especially of a spouse and children who are still growing and developing as we are."[5]

I also suspect that many of us are critical of our spouses without intending to be.

"Many women," according to Patricia Love and Steven Stosny, authors of *How to Improve Your Marriage Without Talking About It,* "have no clue how critical and demeaning they are to men. When confronted with their critical behavior, the most common reaction is disbelief. 'I'm just trying to make him a better person'—that is, more thoughtful, considerate, responsible, reliable, and so on." The authors then list a few dozen ways to "shame a man without trying," including these:

Excluding him from important decisions: "**I told my sister we would vacation with them this year.**"

Correcting what he said: "**It was last Wednesday, not Thursday.**"

Questioning his judgment: "**Are you going to cook those eggs one at a time?**"

Ignoring his advice: "**This is woman's stuff— you really don't know anything about it.**"

Implying inadequacy: "**I wish you had been at that workshop with me**" (not because he would have enjoyed it but because it would have "corrected some of his flaws").

Making unrealistic demands of his time and energy: **"After you rotate the tires and paint the shed, I want you to listen to how my day was."**

Valuing others' needs over his: **Saying to a friend, "Oh, he's not too tired to come and pick you up and then take you back home after we have a nice visit."**

Belittling his work: **"Just what is it you do all day?"**

Ignoring his needs (basically sending the message that they're not important): **"You're not that tired; anyway, having company will give you energy."**

Showing little or no interest in his interests: **"I can't imagine what you see in that."**

Criticizing his family: **"Your sister didn't even offer to help clean up the kitchen!"**

Expecting him to make me happy: **"If we just did more fun things together . . ."**[6]

I chose only a dozen out of the fifty examples they listed, but I got the point in a hurry. It's easy to be critical without intending to be. Of course, the statements above go both ways—in fact, I think I'm guilty of similar offenses in my own marriage. Oops! But that's why we're talking—to see if we can make our own marriages stronger, no matter how humbling the process may be. Before something comes out of our mouth, it's always a good idea to ask, "How will this make my spouse feel? Is my comment really a veiled criticism?"

The only time, the *only* time, when criticism or correction might be acceptable is when it's invited—and even then, it must be given with the guidance of the Holy Ghost, with an attitude of long-suffering, gentleness, meekness, love unfeigned, and kindness (see D&C 121:41–42).

One Chapter, 285 Years

Fourth Nephi is only 49 verses long, but it covers almost 300 years.

Question: Why is it so short?
Answer: Nothing to report.

The children of Lehi had been told numerous times, "If ye will keep my commandments ye shall prosper in the land" (Alma 37:13; see also 1 Nephi 2:20; Mosiah 1:7). They did, and they prospered, for three centuries. Then they grew contentious again and returned to wickedness. End of chapter.

My Book of Mormon class noticed an important repetition in Fourth Nephi. Four times, the phrase "no contention" appears (verses 2, 13, 15, 18). How did they do that? Perhaps they had no contention because they didn't get married? No, that's not it—in fact, it says "they were married, and given in marriage" (verse 11). So here we have an entire society of families and marriages without any contention. Remarkable!

An eternal marriage could last even longer than 300 years, and one of the best keys as to how to accomplish that kind of longevity is given in 4 Nephi 1:15. But before I print the verse, I'd like to show you what it didn't say . . .

And it came to pass that there was no contention in the land, because of the *criticism of the spouses one to another*.

*"One of the remarkable qualities
about God's love for us is that not
only do we experience it as validating
and affirming, but it also produces
growth and **change** in us. It literally
moves us forward, toward Him
and our own eventual exaltation.
It is a sculpting, correcting,
and purposeful kind of love."*

—*Virginia H. Pearce*[7]

Of course, we already know that criticism doesn't work. Let's try another:

> And it came to pass that there was no contention in the land, because of the *communication skills practiced by the people.*

Communication skills are great, but they are no substitute for Christlike attributes. Everyone knows how to talk and how to listen, especially when they're dating. But being willing to listen with a humble heart, and being willing to ask, "Did I do something wrong? Will you forgive me?" is a different matter. Here's another thing 4 Nephi 1:15 doesn't say:

> And it came to pass that there was no contention in the land, *because each spouse was doing his or her duty perfectly.*

Well, perhaps they were doing their duty, but wouldn't that behavior be the result of a change in a deeper place? What would make them *want* to do their duty, with the best of motives? The answer is here, and it is the antidote for contention in marriages, in families, and in society:

> And it came to pass that there was no contention in the land, *because of the love of God which did dwell in the hearts of the people.* (4 Nephi 1:15; emphasis added)

These people loved God. They had internalized the gospel to a very high degree, and it shaped their whole society. What exactly does "the love of God" mean? It could have meaning in three dimensions: Love *for* God (our love for him), love *from* God (his love for us), and love *like* God's (a quality of love).[8] I suspect that the children of Lehi described in Fourth Nephi experienced the love of God in all those ways.

The "thus we see" message from Fourth Nephi is that the best way to help a marriage is not with worldly fixes but with heavenly help. Dr. Douglas E. Brinley has written:

The Lord's solution to our marital problems seems to be this: If we can build the "love of God" into our hearts, there will be no contention or arguing between married partners or between family members. Such contention would be too petty, too inconsequential, given our eternal possibilities. Such a perspective or vision would allow us to establish Zion in our homes, wards, and stakes and to extend righteousness into the entire community.[9]

When Jesus was asked, "Which is the great commandment in the law?" He answered, "Thou shalt love the Lord thy God with all thy heart, and with all thy soul, and with all thy mind. This is the first and great commandment. And the second is like unto it, Thou shalt love thy neighbour as thyself" (Matthew 22:36–39). It's interesting that the first three words of both of the two most important commandments are "Thou shalt *love*."

Obviously, the love of God and the spirit of contention cannot coexist. If we truly desire change and growth for ourselves and our spouses, then in our own homes, and in our own marriages, we can begin every single day by asking ourselves, *What can I do today to bring the Spirit of the Lord and the love of God into my home and into my marriage?*

But Isn't It My Job to Improve My Husband?

~~~

We've all heard the old saying, "Behind every good man is a good woman." We've also heard a few humorous variations, such as, "Behind every good man is a surprised mother-in-law."

People used to ask Camilla Kimball what it was like to be married to a prophet. "I didn't marry a prophet," she would respond, "I married a young returned missionary."[10] Similarly, I have heard Sister Ardeth Kapp tell of some young sister missionaries asking her about her husband, their mission president, "How did you ever find a man like that?" Sister Kapp responded, "I didn't *find* him like this." Perhaps many women have felt that part of a wife's duty and mission is to make her husband into the man he can and should be.

You've probably heard the old observation, "Men hope their wives will stay just the way they were the day they got married. Women, on the other hand, marry their husbands and then hope to transform them into what they want their husbands to be." Often, that pressure from a well-meaning wife to persuade her husband to change and grow is perceived as "nagging." Wendy Watson Nelson has joked, "It's not nagging, it's continuous encouragement."

So the answer is, yes—we're supposed to grow together and help each other become better. The only problem is, what a wife might consider to be "continuous encouragement" often sounds to the husband like "perpetual dissatisfaction." And that's why frustrated husbands often say

"You had better marry the person who has the built-in characteristics you desire because marriage is not a place where you will be able to change another or to fit him/her into the mold of what you want."

—*Elder Hugh W. Pinnock*[11]

things like, "I can't ever do anything right in your eyes," or, "Oh boy, what have I done now?"

It might just be that one of the keys to helping your husband grow into the man he's capable of becoming is to love and accept the man he is right now. On the other hand, one surefire way to discourage him and stifle his growth is to compare him with other husbands and fathers you know. Women don't like to be compared to other women, and men don't like to suffer from comparisons either. Joni Hilton has written:

> I've had non-members express amazement at the bigger-than-life quality of many of the male church members they've met. They recognize that these are men who really have conquered the natural man, and who are Christ-centered. Observers see fabulous dads, devoted husbands, men with strength of character, genuine charity, and a gentleness of heart that's rare in this world. As members, we get used to these "giants" in every ward and

stake, and those who fall short really stand out—maybe that's what makes so many sisters frustrated; they see Sister So-and-So's model husband and want that for their own marriages. And maybe that's why so many brothers go into hiding—it's easier than trying to "compete" with such a high standard. The great news is that the restored gospel is where both can get what they want—we can see others' examples and use them for inspiration, instead of as measuring sticks that show how far we fall short. We can grow more Godlike as we serve in this Kingdom, than anywhere else on earth. When you think of it this way, what a blessing it is to be surrounded by such great examples.[12]

Criticism won't work, comparing won't work, and complaining won't work. Accepting him as he is just might. In short, a man who knows he has the love of his wife today, in spite of his weaknesses, wants to become better for her tomorrow.

First Things First

Okay, Brother Bytheway, I'm with you so far, but our husbands are supposed to lead out in the home. They're supposed to be the patriarchs, to lead our families in doing what the prophets have asked! Are you suggesting we never even bring this up?

Yes, we are getting a little off-track here, but I believe it is vital to start with these building blocks:

What we're hoping for is a change of heart, and a change of behavior to follow.

The Spirit is the only one who can bring that kind of change.

Criticism offends the Spirit.

Therefore, criticism doesn't work!

Conclusion: We must stop doing things that offend the Spirit—criticizing, resenting, withholding forgiveness, focusing on faults. Letting those things go will increase our spiritual power and make the Spirit more present in our marriage.

Okay, so we're going to abandon the criticism. If criticizing doesn't work, then what does work?

Well, we're going to look at some suggestions from Church leaders, marriage counselors, and many others who have written or spoken on the subject. Hopefully, their ideas and experiences will be helpful to you.

Someone once said, "A problem identified is a problem solved."

To help us move toward a solution, we need to know more than just what we want to have happen. We need to know why it isn't happening

"The first key in solving any problem is to diagnose it correctly. You wouldn't bring in a cardiologist if you had a foot problem. You wouldn't bring in an ophthalmologist if you had a back problem. You wouldn't bring in a plumber if the roof leaked, or an electrician if your car was out of gas. Neither would you attempt to solve a skill or competency problem with a value solution; or a motivational problem with a skill or training solution; or a value problem with a motivational solution."

—Stephen R. Covey[13]

in the first place. Is it a *value* problem, a *motivation* problem, or a *competency* problem?

For example, in my work with young men, I have often stressed the importance of going on a mission. I have described missionary work as a great privilege, as a priesthood responsibility, and as a way of paying tithing on one's life. My efforts focused on the "rightness" of serving the Lord. On one occasion a young man said to me, "I know I should go on a mission, but I'm afraid I just can't talk to people. I'm not very good at that." At that point I realized that not everyone has the same concerns. His was not a *value* problem—he knew serving a mission was the right thing to do. It was a *competency* problem—he didn't think he was capable of doing it. Because I hadn't accurately understood how he felt, I was addressing a competency problem with a value solution.

Let's apply this same thinking to the issue of taking the lead in family home evening. For some, it could be a value problem. Perhaps some fathers don't push family home evening because in their own family, a weekly home evening was never seen as necessary or valued as very important. They may be of the opinion, "Well, we rarely had home evening when I was growing up, and we all turned out just fine." What can be done about this? No easy answers. First, keep sending him to the priesthood session of general conference, where I suspect he'll hear someone address the topic of priesthood leadership in the home. You may have to find ways to help him see the value in home evening, scripture study, and family prayer. Make sure he notices what it does for the children. If you can, get the children involved in asking for these important activities.

Some fathers may believe that family home evening is important, but they just don't want to make it happen. This is a *motivation* problem. Perhaps they're exhausted at the end of a busy Monday. Perhaps they've seen too many family home evenings turn into arguments, or they figure it's impossible to get everyone together anyway. Some fathers say, "We're a family, we're all home, therefore it's family home evening, right? Can't we just watch football together?" Perhaps some fathers have watched their wives take over those duties for so long that they're more than happy to let their wives take over. (We'll cover that possibility in more detail later.)

The last one, a competency problem, might be more common than we think, and perhaps the hardest problem for some men to admit.

Anything I Can Do,
My Wife Can Do Better

Some husbands might have a competency problem. In other words, they might feel incompetent regarding leadership in spiritual activities at home. Perhaps they're new in the Church, still learning the gospel, or a little worried that what they have to offer might not measure up to their wives' expectations. Perhaps they've tried to lead out, but their efforts failed, or they were told they were doing it wrong, and they felt embarrassed and stupid. So it's easier to just avoid having family home evening.

I'll happily admit that my wife is simply better at some things than I am. She can whip up a simple lesson, complete with visual aids, in no time. I marvel at her ability to come up with a great learning activity for children ages 8 months, 2, 4, 6, 8, and 10 almost instantly, and then pull it off beautifully.

One time, she made a garbage can and a large mouth out of construction paper. After taping them to the fireplace mantel, she filled a plastic bag with pictures of food items. Then, pulling the items out one at a time, she taught the children where each food item should go. The fruits and vegetables went in the mouth, of course, but the beer, tobacco, and junk food went in the garbage can. What a great Word of Wisdom lesson for kids! I'm afraid I would have opened to Section 89 and bored them to death.

I am not in competition with my wife. We, together, are in competition with the worldly influences that threaten our family. Elder Neal A.

Maxwell taught, "Brethren, marry someone who is your better in some respects; and, sisters, do likewise, so that your eternal partnership is one of compensating competencies."[14]

To be honest, I don't think my wife expects me to do a lesson every week. In fact, I think she knows that she's better at putting such things together than I am (since her lessons always go better than mine). What she does expect from me is *support*. She expects that I will call the children together, that I will drop what I'm doing and be there, that the children will see that this is important to *me,* and that I will help with whatever talents I have. And perhaps that is the key—*I know exactly what my wife's expectations are*. She's not asking me to do everything. She wants me to do what I can do, and to give her the feeling of support. On some occasions, she wants me to do more—but that's the point. I know her expectations week by week. I don't have to read her mind. I know exactly what she wants.

*"For to will is present with me;
but how to perform that
which is good I find not."*

—*Romans 7:18*

What Do You Expect?

With a family going ten different directions at once, taking the lead can be a little tougher for some men than it sounds. One husband found his ideal role in the following way:

> I'm supposed to be the spiritual leader and patriarchal father in the home, so I tried to get the children together for family prayer. And my wife said, 'Well, honey, it's probably not a good time right now. In about five minutes one of the kids will be home, and another child is just finishing his homework

assignment and . . ." I don't know how many times I tried to gather the family, to no avail. So at a certain point I thought, Never mind, I'm not going to try. Every time I try I get put down. . . . My first inclination was to say, "Fine. Why don't you just wear the pants in the family?" Though I saw my role as patriarch hanging in the balance, I let go of my pride a little and said, "Honey, I don't always know when the best time is, but I would appreciate your support on this. So why don't you suggest when a good time would be, and then I'll call everyone to family prayer." It worked. My initial problem with her suggesting anything was the sense that if she had to remind me, I must be a failure. The problem was that I was interpreting her "suggestion" as a sign of my inadequacy. And it's not about being inadequate; it's about working together and letting her be a helpmate. It's about being supportive.[15]

As mentioned before, you might want to clarify in detail what your expectations are with your spouse. My wife has her hand on the pulse of the family, and when she can tell me exactly what she expects of me, as a task-oriented male, I can do it.

So, as a wife, what do you imagine family home evening to be? And what does your husband's being a leader in the home look like to you? Calling the family together? Assigning the lesson? Giving the lesson? Supporting you as you or one of the children gives the lesson? Does your husband know these expectations?

Perhaps you could take the "reminder" role and ask him to be the "initiator." Or, if you're better at tracking where everyone is, you could be the "initiator," and he could be the "supporter." It has been said that frustrations come from unmet expectations, so if you want to avoid frustration, define the roles that work for both of you, then make sure your expectations are known!

De-fense! (clap, clap)
De-fense! (clap, clap)

I f you need to clarify your expectations with
your husband, then you might need to talk to
him about it. Uh-oh. Three of the most frightening
words a man may ever hear are these: "Can we
talk?" (which is strange, since most women *love* to
hear those words). Dr. John Lund explains why:

> When a woman approaches a man, his first
> reaction tends to be defensive. "What do you
> want from me now? I am the guardian of my
> time. Do you want some of my time?" . . .
> There [are] three things men [want] to know

when engaging in a conversation with a woman:

1. Is this going to be painful?
2. How long is this going to take?
3. What do you want from me when this conversation is over?

A number of women have said to me, "I think that for men to be defensive is silly. Why don't they just get over it and grow up?" Women who think this way are living on the wrong planet. What they are really saying is that men need to be more like women. That's true until you need men to be warriors. There are two kinds of warriors: defensive warriors and dead warriors. Good luck, ladies, expecting your men not to be defensive. The idea that men are monotaskers is a good thing. It makes them good warrior-protectors and providers. Now, let me ask the women, Do you want your warrior-protector out there when he's sword-fighting and defending you to be thinking, "I wonder if my wife wants that small couch downstairs"? Those men aren't with us anymore. They're all dead. And if you saw the movie, *The Princess Bride,* they are not mostly dead, but dead dead. It serves the male gender well to be focused. But it is also true that men are capable of improvement and could work on being less defensive with the women in their lives.[16]

Men and women are different, and personally, I'm delighted with the differences. We perceive things differently, we react differently, and we converse differently—in fact, *we actually talk for different reasons.* This realization has helped me a great deal in my relationship with my wife and the other women in my life. The difference in our communication needs has been summarized by author Deborah Tannen in one sentence: "Men talk for information, women talk for interaction."[17] It's true.

When I was in college, I remember showing up unexpectedly once at my parents' house. My mom sat me down and with great animation started explaining in detail what every one of my siblings was up to. I listened for a while, and then I became a little frustrated because I couldn't seem to figure out why she was telling me all this. I was saying inside, "There must be something in here I need to know."

Later, I learned the little truth stated above: "Men talk for information, women talk for inter-action." I was listening for information, but my mom wasn't just relaying information, she was interacting—she was strengthening the relationship. We talk for different reasons!

As a new husband, if my wife told me about something that was wrong, my first inclination was to fix it. Why? Because I thought she was giving me a problem to solve. I had a chance to save the day! I could be a hero in her eyes. Today I realize that my real job is to listen and empathize. I've become much better at nodding, gasping in the right spots, and adding little comments like, "No way!" and "You must have been mortified."

Every cell in my body wants to suggest solutions and move on to my next task, but that's not my job. Thankfully, my wife knows to tell me up front if she needs a problem solver or a nodding empathizer. It's still tough for me, but hey—a man's gotta do what a man's gotta do.

Now, back to the matter at hand: When you talk to your husband about your expectations, and about being more of a leader in the home, you need to let him know that this time, you need more than an empathizer—you need a problem solver. Additionally, remember that *how* you ask is just as important as what you say. I'm certain you know exactly how to approach this, but in case you're wondering, here's a suggestion: Take both of his hands in yours, gaze lovingly into his eyes, and say, "Honey, would you do something for me?" Boy, will you have his attention.

Now, what should you ask for, or how exactly should you put your request into words? That's coming up next.

You Want Me to *What?!*

I heard something once that astounded me because of how true it was, although I'd never been able to articulate it before. As soon as my wife and I understood this fact about men, it immediately blessed our marriage.

Here it is: *Men look for exits.* In a study done at the University of Washington, fifty men and fifty women gathered into a large building and were asked for their opinions on some issue. A week later, the same group was invited back and asked to remember something totally unrelated to the issue mentioned the week before. The question they were asked was, "Which direction was north from where you were seated in that building, and where were the exits in that room?"

The results were fascinating.

Less than 20 percent of the women knew where any of the exits were. Over 80 percent of the men nailed every exit in the building and knew where north was. What is there about men that they are aware of exits? Why are men accused of having a hard time committing? It's because men are reluctant to commit until they can see an exit or clearly understand the boundaries. The more open-ended something is, the more difficult it is for a man to commit.[18]

This is wonderful insight, a wonderful tool, that you can use tonight!

Asking a man to take out the garbage is one thing. Asking him to change his life is another.

"Nothing is particularly difficult if you divide it into small jobs."

—Henry Ford

"How to Get a Man to Listen: *Make a time, give him an agenda, announce a time limit, and tell him you don't want solutions or plans of action. Say, 'I'd like to talk with you about my day. Would after dinner be okay? I don't need any solutions to problems—I'd just like you to listen.' Most men will agree to a request like this because it has a time, a place, and an objective—all the things that appeal to the male brain. And he is not expected to do any work.*"

—Barbara and Allan Pease[19]

Asking specifically for what you need *at the moment* is vastly different from asking for a life-long, qualitative transformation.

To demonstrate, which sounds more daunting to you?

"Will you take the lead in all family spiritual responsibilities for the rest of your natural life?"

Or

"Honey, I need your help for forty-five minutes tonight, starting at 6:30"?

The second one sounds a little less over-whelming, doesn't it? It gives him a time and an "exit," and he knows he's not being asked to exalt the family before SportsCenter. If you make your requests with a built-in exit strategy, they might be more effective.

This is why bottomless "Honey-Do" lists can be discouraging to men. They never know when they're finished—there's not an exit in sight! One husband told me, "Whenever my wife sees me doing something I really want to do, she immediately thinks of something else she thinks I ought to be doing."

Whenever you make a request, try designating an exit. Be specific. Since men tend to be task-oriented, they will respond better when they know exactly what you want them to do and when their task will be done. Admittedly, this may not solve the larger problem, but it's a step in the right direction. It's a small insight that, used repeatedly, can lead to a big result.

Don't Ask Him to Resign

Some men—only a few, I hope—have resigned their leadership because they feel they've been asked to. Listen to this composite dialogue between a marriage counselor and a wife who's frustrated with her husband's lack of leadership.

Mrs. Jones: You know, he's just not the man he used to be.

Dr. Welby: Explain that.

Mrs. Jones: He doesn't take charge like he

used to; he's become very lazy. He just sits back and lets me decide everything.

Dr. Welby: Why do you suppose he would do that?

Mrs. Jones: I guess he's just lazy and wants me to do everything, and that's why we're here.

Dr. Welby: I asked your husband to describe what happened the last time you went out together. I've condensed some of what he said, but as I review some of the events of that evening, I'd like you to listen for a pattern. See if you see what I see.

Mrs. Jones: Okay.

Dr. Welby: Let's see, you told him: you're driving too fast; you'd better change lanes; we could have been there by now if you'd . . . ; why didn't you park closer; why didn't you ask for a better table . . .

Mrs. Jones: That's not how it happened!

Dr. Welby: I'm editing. I realize there were other things said in between, I'm just selecting certain parts of your conversation and wondering if you're seeing a pattern.

Mrs. Jones: Well, he always drives too aggressively, and he did park in a bad spot, and—

Dr. Welby: That may be true, but I want you to discover something that may be related to your husband's lack of leadership.

Mrs. Jones: Okay.

Dr. Welby: Here are a few more things he heard that night: you should have given her a better tip; did you remember to turn on the lights? I could go on, but are you noticing anything in here?

Mrs. Jones: Well, you've just taken certain statements out of context.

Dr. Welby: Perhaps. Does this sort of thing happen at home as well?

Mrs. Jones: I know what you think—you think I criticize too much.

Dr. Welby: What I think is not important, it's what your husband thinks and feels . . .

Mrs. Jones: I just wish he'd . . . I'm just trying to help him become the man he should be.

Dr. Welby: I think your husband, although he's not accustomed to expressing his feelings—

Mrs. Jones: He doesn't express anything.

Dr. Welby: But I think your husband *has* feelings, and he, like all of us, just wants to be valued and respected.

Mrs. Jones: I respect him.

Dr. Welby: Considering the messages, verbal and otherwise, you sent him that night about driving too fast, not choosing the right parking place, not tipping correctly, et cetera, would you say those messages would make him feel important and admired?

Mrs. Jones: No, but he gets plenty of that at work, he—

Dr. Welby: Exactly.

Mrs. Jones: What?

Dr. Welby: Where is the place, in fact the *only* place, where your husband really, consistently

"When a woman criticizes a man, whether she does it deliberately or not, she makes it impossible for him to feel connected to her. Where there is a withdrawn or silent man, there is usually a critical woman."

—*Patricia Love and Steven Stosny*[20]

feels respected and admired? You answered the question. Is it in his marriage, or is it in his career? When he goes to the office, he's respected for his competency. He's not questioned about every little decision. He's admired for what he has done and for what he's doing. He's treated well by his administrative assistant and his boss, and by the staff too. He's appreciated. And he seems to have no trouble exercising leadership and prerogative there.

I've seen it dozens of times. What if he is drawn to the admiration and respect of a woman? Will he find it at home, or at the office? A lot of affairs and a lot of divorces begin just this way.

Let me ask you another question. Do you ever hear your husband say to your children, "Go ask your mother"?

Mrs. Jones: Yes, all the time.

Dr. Welby: Why do you think he does that?

Mrs. Jones: Because, like I said before, he's lazy, and he wants me to do everything.

Dr. Welby: That could be part of it. Or maybe it's because he feels that if he makes any decision, you'll just tell him that it's wrong. It's easier to send the children to you in the first place rather than make a decision, take some leadership, and have his decision reversed later on.

Every little criticism, every little barb, chips away at his leadership, and it also takes away a little of his manhood. The course of least resistance, which is what men often look for, is to just let you have your way. They merely want peace in the family. When a chance to show leadership emerges, it's also another risk for him to be shot down. So he resigns. You're lucky, Mrs. Jones—some husbands leave. Your husband didn't leave, he just resigned. He gave up his leadership role and said, "I resign, go ask your mother."

Soon, he will start asking you where you want to park, and where you want to sit, and what you think the tip should be, because being told "you did it wrong" is just too hard on his ego, and he'd rather avoid the fight. And instead of molding a man who leads, you've created a man who looks to you to make every decision.

I'm here to tell you that yes, your husband could be a better leader, a take-charge kind of guy, but without knowing it, you've been asking for his resignation for years. And I don't know how long ago it was, but he finally gave up and turned it in.

Mrs. Jones: So what do you want me to do?

Dr. Welby: What do you think would help your marriage?

Mrs. Jones: You want me to stop criticizing him.

Dr. Welby: I want what you want, to salvage your marriage, which means cutting down on criticism, but that's not accurate enough. I want you to listen carefully to the messages you send him every day, and ask yourself if they're messages that build him up or tear him down. That is not going to be easy, because this correcting appears to be a pattern, a habit. If you think you can't change, you'd better decide how much you value your marriage.

We've talked about feelings. Now let's talk about facts:

Fact: This man wanted to marry you. He chose you!

Fact: He asked you to be his wife!

Fact: He is still with you!

Fact: He is willing to see a marriage counselor to make things better. That's huge.

How did you treat him when you were dating? My guess is that you admired him—you thought he was the greatest guy on earth. Can you treat him like that again, even though you know him better now? Can you send messages of admiration every day? I believe many of his leadership qualities will reemerge when you let him lead. Some things, like reckless driving, are important. But some things just don't matter. This is your choice. Do you really want to risk bringing a toxic tone into your marriage over things like parking spaces, or a 15 percent tip that should have been 20 percent?

Wow. I hesitated to share that dialogue, because it's an extreme example—at least I *hope* it's extreme. Some wives ask their husbands to resign their leadership role. Maybe they don't realize that is what they're doing, but every time a wife questions her husband's decisions, she is essentially asking for his resignation.

Hopefully, this has nothing to do with your particular situation, but it's good for all of us to review the things we say every day to our spouses. Sister Wendy Watson Nelson suggests that our positive, encouraging messages should outnumber our negative messages by a ratio of five to one.

Researchers have become very interested in determining the ratio of positive to negative communication between spouses that will keep a marriage on a pathway of improvement and increased happiness. The magic ratio they have found is five to one. That is, as long as there is at least five times more affection, humor, smiling, complimenting, agreement, empathy, and active listening than there is criticism and disagreement, your marriage will prosper. (See Gottman and Silver, *Why Marriages Succeed or Fail.*) What does the ratio in your marriage look like? Again, repetition and consistency are important. Having a five-to-one ratio of positive to negative communication only on Sundays will not strengthen your marriage through the rest of the week—let alone through the rest of your lives.[21]

Another way to look at this information is to realize that for every negative comment you make, you will have to make five positive comments to erase its effects and break even. It's a lot easier to never make the negative comment to begin with. You might try to determine the ratio of positive to negative communication in your own marriage. It might be difficult to explain why you're carrying a clipboard around, but it will be worth it. "Strengthen your brethren in all your conversation," the Lord taught in Doctrine and Covenants 108:7, "in all your prayers, in all your exhortations, and in all your doings." Surely we can apply this counsel to our marriages as well as our other relationships.

We are all familiar with the golden rule, "Do unto others, as you would have them do unto you." We're also acquainted with King Benjamin's advice: "When ye are in the service of your fellow beings ye are only in the service of your God" (Mosiah 2:17). And all of us know the story of the Good Samaritan who was "neighbor" to the man who fell among thieves (see Luke 10:30–37). Lastly, we sing with gusto, "Let us oft speak kind words to each other."[22] The odd thing is, when we attempt to apply these scriptures and principles to our lives, we're usually thinking about "other people": the family down the street, the guy at work, or the woman who needed help getting her groceries into the trunk. Why don't we apply these scriptures to our marriages? Our marriages should be the *first* place we implement these ideas, not the last. Our spouses are our neighbors, our fellow beings, and the others to whom we should be speaking kind words.

Men Are Simple Creatures

As I type those words, I can almost hear a female chorus respond, "You can say that again."

As a husband of thirteen years, I think I can speak for many men when I say that what I really want from my wife is simply to be respected and admired. Personally, I crave that.

The famous actress Katharine Hepburn once said, "If you want to sacrifice the admiration of many men for the criticism of one, go ahead, get married."[23] That's a humorous statement with a sad aftertaste. Is that what marriage is? Trading the admiration you received from many people, when you were single, for the criticism of the one person you chose to spend eternity with? Yuck! What kind of arrangement is that? Why would anyone want that? For eternity?!

If home is just a place where you are constantly reminded of your shortcomings, why would you want to be there? You might be tempted to work late if you knew that when you got home you were just going to get hit with a list of all the things you hadn't done and all the ways you were inadequate.

Although most men would not admit it or talk too much about it, the respect and admiration they desire are under continual attack—sometimes by themselves!

Most husbands are under constant economic pressure to support a wife and children. . . . Such husbands are faced not only with the daily realities of being able to provide food,

*"It should come as no great surprise
to wives that husbands want to be
loved, more so than anything else."*

—*Dr. Brent A. Barlow*[24]

clothing, and housing for their families, but with the knowledge that in a society in which many are reasonably well off, they are not.

A man's self-image in our society is deeply affected by his ability to provide for his family. Many times, the self-image is not too positive.[25]

One morning, I had an early appointment to keep, and I had to get up when it was still dark outside. As I walked into the bathroom, I noticed that my wife had taped a note to the shower door. It wasn't a "be sure to . . ." or a "don't forget, you promised to . . ." note. It was short, simple, and amazingly powerful: "I just hope you know how much I love you and how much I appreciate these heroic lengths you go to to provide for us." The impact of those few words was immediate. I felt appreciated, I felt respected, and I felt admired. I also felt motivated to work even harder to make myself the man of my wife's dreams.

My wife knows my faults. She knows my shortcomings. She could have reminded me to work on any one of them that morning. But I left the house feeling like the luckiest man alive because I have a wife who admires me. (She even used the word *heroic*—did you notice that?) And rather than dreading coming home at the end of the day to face a tired, frustrated-with-all-the-kids wife, I couldn't wait for my hero's welcome.

Roy, a caller to the *Dr. Laura* radio program, commented:

If you can't accentuate the positive, at least acknowledge it. The world is full of messages to men that there are standards we don't meet. There is always another man who is more handsome, more virile, or more athletic than we are. None of that matters if the most important person in our life looks up to us, accepts us as we are, and loves us even though we aren't perfect.

Maybe there is a part of the small boy that never leaves the grown man, I don't know. All I know is that the husband who has a wife who supports him and praises him for the positive things he does is the envy of all the other men who have to live with criticism, sarcasm, and constant reminders of their failures.[26]

If it's really true that men simply want to be admired, and I believe it is, then we have another key to blessing your marriage. If every wife, before engaging in a conversation or making a request of her spouse, could ask herself, "How will this help my husband feel respected and admired?" and then adjust her approach appropriately, it could have a huge impact on the health of the relationship.

Now, here's the kiss of death: One father, in a sincere effort to help out his wife, dressed the children and got them ready for church. He didn't do the girls' hair perfectly or match their clothes just right, and he later learned that the Relief Society had been told, "My husband dressed the kids today, and do you know what he did?"

Question—would this make him feel respected and admired? Or did he feel like a laughingstock? Perhaps some husbands could laugh such a thing off, but this one didn't. Would he ever want to risk helping out again? Probably not.

Once again, men are simple creatures. Like all of us, they just want their efforts to be respected and admired, even if they don't do things perfectly.

Praising Betimes with Sharpness

When your husband's leadership potential comes out, does he hear about it?

We're all familiar with the phrase "reproving betimes with sharpness" from Doctrine and Covenants 121:43. What does "sharpness" mean? Elder H. Burke Peterson taught: "Reproving with sharpness means reproving with clarity, with loving firmness, with serious intent. It does not mean reproving with sarcasm, or with bitterness, or with clenched teeth and raised voice."[27]

What a helpful insight! The word *sharpness*

implies "clarity," "exactness," or "specificity." Could we utilize that kind of clarity in our praise and encouragement? What would happen, for example, if you made a real effort to praise the specific behavior you'd like to see, rather than criticizing or pointing out the absence of that behavior in a general way?

Imagine the impact a sentence like this could have on a husband: "Honey, you said something to the kids the other day that I loved. Thank you for your influence that way. I wish they could hear you more often." Certainly, you'll get a lot more mileage from that approach than, "Why don't you talk to the kids more? You're supposed to be teaching them as their father!"

Since we've already established that criticism doesn't work and that it offends the Spirit, how about we focus more on being generous in our praise, and in praising specifically the behavior we're hoping to see more of—or, in other words, praising "with sharpness"? One woman suggested:

When you catch him doing even almost the RIGHT things, . . . stop and take more time than usual to tell him how much that particular action means to you. Tell him in almost drawn out detail WHY it meant so much—that it helped you to be relieved of having to promote or gather together the children for prayer; that he didn't HAVE to be called away from the computer game (at least he had gathered them together for the prayer time). *That made the children think they meant more to you than a game.*[28]

Some might say, "That sounds like manipulation." I disagree! Is it manipulation to water the part of the lawn that needs it the most? Is it manipulation to encourage the good in someone rather than pointing out the bad? If so, I can show you a thousand husbands who would love to be manipulated.

Praising others isn't something we do because it works; it's something we do because it's right. I suspect that most of us have sincerely thought of many nice things we could say about our loved ones, but sometimes those thoughts remain in our brains, never making the journey a few inches down to our mouths where they can come out and do some good. All of us could praise a little more, and we could praise with sharpness.

Back when I was single, one of my sisters said something that would greatly bless my future marriage. We had gathered at my parents' home for a large family home evening. She had been through a divorce, and was sitting quietly in the kitchen while my other siblings and their spouses were enjoying an energetic discussion. An older brother-in-law was going on and on in glowing terms about his wife (one of my older sisters) and the job she had done with the stake choir. Suddenly, someone noticed tears welling up in my younger sister's eyes. The discussion quieted, and finally someone asked, "What's wrong?" I will never forget her answer: "I'm just wondering what

*"The grass isn't greener
on the other side;
the grass is greener
where you water it."*

*—A guy named Mel, from
Intermountain Sprinkler*

it would be like to have a husband talk about me like that." You could have heard a pin drop. As I mentioned, I wasn't married at the time, but I took a vow right then and there that my future wife would *never* say that. She would never have to sit and wonder what it would be like to have her husband praise her and say nice things about her in the presence of others.

I think you know where I'm going with this, because it works both ways. Has your husband ever wondered what it would be like to have his wife say wonderful things about him in public? If so, you know exactly how to fix that. Elder Joe J. Christensen and his wife, Barbara, were given some personal advice by President Spencer W. Kimball:

> Don't ever be critical of each other, even in jest. Never run each other down—especially in the presence of others—because sooner or later one of you will get your feelings hurt and it won't be a joke anymore. Always build each

other. Compliment each other in the presence
of your friends and you will reap great rewards
in your companionship.[29]

It goes without saying that we should be
fiercely loyal to our spouses. I should feel confident, for example, that when my wife goes to
enrichment night, she's not talking about my failures or foibles with the other women of the ward,
and she should feel confident that her failures are
not a topic at the high priest social. I don't expect
my wife to say *nothing* about our marriage and
our lives to others. That wouldn't be reasonable.
But part of our loyalty to each other is the confi-
dence and assurance we feel in knowing that if
one of us is out talking about the other one, it
will only be in positive ways. I believe that if you
will make it a habit to praise your husband "with
sharpness" in public, it will have a marvelous
effect back in the privacy of your home.

Will You Plant Your Tulips Next to Mine?

Sometimes my wife gives me notes. Sometimes I respond by giving her fragrant flora. Flowers have a wonderful effect on my wife—they change the whole day. Along with the appreciation I see on her face (and the accompanying hug and kiss), I've also noticed that she changes toward me, and I change toward her. We're more patient with each other through the day; we're a little bit nicer, and a little bit more forgiving. *We want the feeling to stay.* Sometimes the feeling only lingers for a day or two, but hey, what's wrong with having a nice spirit in the home for a day or two? (Long enough for the flowers to wilt, so that I can bring home some more, right?)

Which leads me to conclude that *the more we act in kind and loving ways toward others, the more others will act in kind and loving ways toward us*. I'll bet you can recall a time in your marriage when something like this happened. A kindness given by one spouse was soon returned by the other. If not, try the experiment yourself today. Write a little note of appreciation to your husband, and see if he doesn't change a little toward you that day.

Here's the point—you may have noticed that a certain word has already been used four times in this section. The word is *change*. And isn't that what we want? A change of heart? What was true earlier in the book is still true now—rarely is anyone criticized into changing. But they just might be loved and appreciated into changing.

When my wife does something thoughtful for

"[Pride] is manifest in so many ways, such as faultfinding, gossiping, backbiting, murmuring, living beyond our means, envying, coveting, withholding gratitude and praise that might lift another, and being unforgiving and jealous."

—*President Ezra Taft Benson*[30]

me, of course, I appreciate it. But something else always happens. I want to be better for her today than I was yesterday.

I Think I'll Be Delightful Today

❧❧❧

My wife and I had a wonderful, once-in-a-lifetime opportunity to go on a Mediterranean cruise. We were part of a small group of about twenty-five Latter-day Saints, and upon our first meeting, we each introduced ourselves.

I will never forget the introduction of one couple. A woman rose to her feet and said, "My name is Donna, and this is my husband, Ken. I just love traveling with Ken. He's just so fun to be with, and I'm so happy to be here with him." A few more times during our cruise activities,

Donna repeated publicly how much she just *loved* traveling with her husband, Ken, and how much she enjoyed being with him. On each of these occasions, Ken just sat there with a pleasant look on his face. During the next two weeks, I learned that Donna was right. Ken *was* delightful to be with. But did he start out that way, or was he just eager to prove his wife right by living up to her expectations? I don't know. Perhaps a little of both.

I remember thinking several times, "Would Kim say that about me? Am I fun to be with?" Odd as it might sound, there are frequently somewhat stressful situations on a cruise (particularly when you have children with you). You have to get off the ship at a certain time, find a bus for a certain excursion, finish up your shopping and rejoin the group, and so forth. I reviewed my own impatience at times, my own frustration when we were the last ones back on board, and such things. I decided I might not be fun to be with when I'm stressed. I also decided I wanted to be more like Ken.

It's been a long time since that cruise, but I still think about that couple. There are many mornings when I'm uptight, sleep deprived, and I've got a billion things to do. But I look at my puffy eyes and my "bed head" in the bathroom mirror and I remember Donna and Ken, and I set myself a goal—I think I'll be delightful. Every day brings new problems, but I can still choose to be delightful. *Anyone* can choose to be delightful.

Will your being delightful change your spouse? I don't know. What do you think? It's pretty hard to stay glum when you're around someone who is fun to be with. But even if it doesn't change anyone else, isn't it downright delightful to be with yourself when you're downright delightful?

Brother Bytheway, I appreciate this cute story, but how will this help my husband take the lead?

Here's how. If I had the chance to sit on that

"I know it is hard for you young mothers to believe that almost before you can turn around the children will be gone and you will be alone with your husband.
You had better be sure you are developing the kind of love and friendship that will be delightful and enduring. Let the children learn from your attitude that he is important. Encourage him. Be kind.
It is a rough world, and he, like everyone else, is fighting to survive.
Be cheerful. Don't be a whiner."

—*Marjorie Pay Hinckley*[31]

Q & A panel again, one rather blunt question I would be tempted to ask is, "How's your marriage?" (But that's not the kind of thing you want to ask a lone sister in front of an audience of a few thousand.) It seems to me that if the marriage is good, issues like taking the lead can normally be discussed and resolved in a cooperative spirit. If the health of the marriage is not so good, perhaps some other things can be done that hopefully, over time, will improve the marriage and help create a better climate for talking about problems, whatever they may be. I am convinced that focusing on improving the marriage is a better strategy than focusing on one partner's weakness in the marriage.

What's Your
Love Language?

~~~

A number of years ago, Dr. Gary Chapman wrote a book entitled *The Five Love Languages,* which categorized the following different ways of expressing love: (1) Quality Time, (2) Words of Affirmation, (3) Gifts, (4) Acts of Service, (5) Physical Touch.[32] He suggested that each of us has a "primary love language," or one we prefer most.

Dr. Chapman's ideas resulted in a very helpful discussion between me and my wife. Early in our marriage, I tried to show her my love by

"Shut Up and Kiss Me"

—*Title of a country music song*

vacuuming out the car. I learned from our discussion that she would prefer "quality time" and "words of affirmation" over tidy transportation. (I still vacuum out the car because, personally, I love tidy transportation—but when I want my *wife* to know I love her, I try to say it in her language.)

What's your husband's primary love language? I suppose a good guess for most men would be "physical touch." Dr. Charles Beckert had an audience of married couples rolling with laughter when he suggested some of the ways wives can reward their husbands. (I transcribed this advice from an audiotape, so you'll just have to imagine where the laughter came in—but I think you'll be able to tell.)

Well, what could I do if I want my husband to be the leader in the family? All I'm saying is don't *tell* him to be the leader. *Encourage* him. If nothing else, and people laugh at this, it's the old behavioral psychology technique how you train rats and pigeons and dogs and cats—but it works on men too. And women too. You reward positive behavior. All you have to do is, in the cupboard, have a bowl of jelly beans—*or any other reward that's important to the husband*. Did I say that right? Okay? You have a bowl of jelly beans, or *any other reward that's important to the husband*. When he behaves like a leader, then you reward him. Okay? And pretty soon he's going to *really* enjoy being the leader. I hope that doesn't sound too corny to you, but I hope you realize there are lots of ways to reward men.[33]

Yup, men are simple creatures. If he loves jelly beans, get a jar of those. If there's something else he really prefers, well, I'll just repeat Dr. Beckert—there are lots of ways to reward men. What's your husband's love language?

Object Lessons Only
Work in Primary

I hesitate to share the following story, but the point is just too good to pass up, so here goes. My very first college roommates shall remain nameless. They were nice guys, but they rarely did their dishes or cleaned the apartment. I found it difficult to study in such a messy place, so I usually cleaned it myself. When I think of those particular roommates, three words come to mind—"bless their hearts" (that's the phrase we use in the Church when we'd really like to say a whole lot more). Now that I've been married for more than a decade, and wondering what they might be up to these days, along with a smile, three different words come to mind: *Their poor wives!*

Anyway, I decided at one point that I would just leave their dishes in the sink until it got stacked so high that suddenly they would have a spontaneous change of heart and say, "You know, guys, we really ought to maintain more of a righteous environment here in our little apartment—I think we should all pitch in and help." So I waited. And waited. And waited. Until mold was growing on the soiled dishes in the sink and the kitchen began to smell. Eventually I caved, cleaned up after them again, sold my contract mid-semester, and moved out. As a final insult, I had to clean the apartment one last time in order to get my security deposit back.

I decided that object lessons didn't work. I also had to adopt the motto, "If it is to be, it is up to me," at least when it came to cleaning the apartment. The question that faces many women in the Church is similar, but with eternal consequences—if family home evening, scripture study, and so on aren't happening in my home, should I just let it go, hoping that my husband will figure it out, or should I do it myself?

Sister Beverly Campbell addressed this very question in her book, *You Don't Need to Slay My Dragons, Just Take Out the Trash:*

> I am often asked: "How do we, as a partnership, translate Church programs, roles, and responsibilities into an active working model in the home?" One young wife told me, only half-jokingly, that if family home evenings were to be held in their home, she had to do all the planning, call the children together, pull her husband away from his computer, and then tell him that everything was ready so he could preside.
>
> Amidst the laughter I sensed her underlying feeling of frustration and even guilt. Was

something wrong with her that the "ideal pattern" was not being played out in her home? Was it right for her to carry so much of the load to make these programs a part of their ongoing family life? And if all this was expected of her, why wasn't she being given a little more control and credit?

Yes, in the ideal situation the priesthood holder will lead out in implementing all of the wonderful safeguard programs that are so much a part of our religion: the family home evenings, family prayer, temple attendance, and so on. But in reality, all of the above becomes work of the partnership.

Elder Neal A. Maxwell recognized that "ideal" is a bit like "fair"; it doesn't always happen. He advised: "Malfunctioning fathers are a much more common phenomenon in the Church than are malfunctioning mothers. Often the success-oriented male leaves untended some of his responsibilities to his wife and family. . . . Having one 'sentry' who has gone AWOL joined by another 'sentry,' the wife and mother, is no help" (*Deposition of a Disciple*, 84).

And therein lies the answer. As a mother in Zion, would you deny yourself, your home, or your family any of the needed and available blessings? You are a full and equal partner. If a child needs a father's blessing, suggest it. If family prayer is being sidetracked, reinstitute it. If family home evenings are going to be fun, you know you can make it happen. Involve your husband as much as you can. Kidnap him if need be—but turn it into a positive rather than a negative experience. Pencil a temple date into his calendar and make it just that—a date. Soon he'll get the spirit of it.

Opt for the greater good regardless of who gets the credit.[34]

To let family home evening, family prayer, and scripture study go undone as an "object lesson" is spiritually risky. My favorite statement in Sister

Campbell's response is "opt for the greater good regardless of who gets the credit." Yes, it would be great if your husband was taking the lead, but for now, let's make sure the children experience the gospel in the home. It will bless them forever. And then keep working on things with a hopeful expectation.

Perhaps your husband is less active, or not a member. Talk to him about what he would be willing to do. Make a deal. For example, "Are you willing to kneel with us? Are you willing to listen in during family home evening?" Find out what's acceptable to him, agree on it, and be happy with that for now. Then move forward with faith and hope for a greater change in the future.

"Strangling Your Husband Is Not an Option"

Merrilee Boyack wrote a helpful marriage book using the above phrase as the title—and she suggests using the "as if" principle to help bring about the change you're looking for:

> Let's just say you've been frustrated with how your husband acts with respect to spiritual things in the home. You would like him to be a better patriarch. . . . So you are going to treat him as if he were a wonderful patriarch in the home—a veritable spiritual giant. You are going to treat him as if he presides in your

home. Okay, so it's time for family prayer. As the family is gathered, you bow your head and keep your mouth shut. The patriarch in the home calls on the person to give the prayer, right? After some uncomfortable moments of quiet (where everyone is peeking at each other wondering what is wrong with mother), your husband will say, "Uh, honey, weren't you going to call on someone to say the prayer?" "Oh, no," you reply, "I realized that that was *your* job as the patriarch in the home. I'm sorry I've been messing up on that. I won't do it again." Now all the kids are rather bug-eyed and glancing at Dad. Dad squares his shoulders and says, "Uh, oh, well then. Uh, Jimmy would you pray?" Never again do you take over at family prayer. And from then on, he will act as the patriarch and call on some-one to pray. . . .

What if, every morning, you began by looking at him and saying to yourself, "He is a wonderful man of God." How would you treat

"Treat a man as he is and he will remain as he is. Treat a man as he can and should be and he will become as he can and should be."

—*Goethe*[35]

him all day? If you kept that thought right there in front of your eyes, how would you act? You can see the major shift in how you would behave, can't you. And yes, for some men this is a huge leap of imagination. But you can pretend. You can relentlessly treat "as if." And over time, not only will he begin to act *as if* he is, but he will *become* that wonderful man of God. And you will believe that he is to the core of your being as well. . . .

Now the reverse can also be true. If you treat your husband as if he is a lazy, irresponsible man, *he might just show you you're right.*[36]

When was the last time you read your husband's patriarchal blessing? (For that matter, when was the last time you read your own?) Sister Boyack's suggestion that you try to view your husband the way God views him is only as far away as his patriarchal blessing (or his "personal scripture,"[37] to use a phrase from President Ezra Taft Benson).

Recently I took the opportunity to reread my wife's blessing and I was immediately humbled, grateful, and a little awestruck. "You're really something, you know that?" I told her as I folded it back up and returned it to the envelope.

As you read your husband's blessing, you'll know that you didn't marry a loser, you married a son of God. Sister Elaine Jack observed:

> What does a patriarchal blessing say? Have you ever heard of one which says, "I am sorry—you're a loser. Do the best you can on earth, and we'll see you in about seventy years." Of course not! And you never will, because of the divine qualities each of God's children has inherited. A patriarchal blessing is like a road map, a guide, directing you in your walk through life. It identifies your talents and the good things that can be yours.[38]

I might suggest that after you've read about your husband's capacity and potential, you might express your feelings to him, and then get him to read it again too. Maybe he could use a reminder of how the Lord sees him as well. It might just be the dose of encouragement and motivation he needs.

Don't Forget
to Remember

My wife and I have D&C 90:24 displayed on the most important, most prominent place in the house—the fridge. It's a wonderful marriage scripture. Two words in this verse are very important to us: *remember* and *covenant*. When we have rough spots in our marriage, which I suppose everyone does, all we have to do is remember our covenant—we know that we are committed to making our temple marriage grow into a celestial marriage.

Occasionally, I have to remind myself that I

"*Search diligently, pray always, and be believing, and all things shall work together for your good, if ye walk uprightly and remember the covenant wherewith ye have covenanted one with another.*"

—D&C 90:24

have not made a covenant with the golf course, college football, or my laptop. I have, however, made a covenant with God, and with my wife. In fact, the three of us are all parties to my most important covenant, my marriage.

Elder Bruce C. Hafen explained the monumental difference between a "contract" marriage and a "covenant" marriage:

> When troubles come, the parties to a *contractual* marriage seek happiness by walking away. They marry to obtain benefits and will stay only as long as they're receiving what they bargained for. But when troubles come to a *covenant* marriage, the husband and wife work them through. They marry to give and to grow, bound by covenants to each other, to the community, and to God. *Contract* companions each give 50 percent; *covenant* companions each give 100 percent.
>
> Marriage is by nature a covenant, not just a private contract one may cancel at will. Jesus

taught about contractual attitudes when he described the "hireling," who performs his conditional promise of care only when he receives something in return. When the hireling "seeth the wolf coming," he "leaveth the sheep, and fleeth . . . because he . . . careth not for the sheep." By contrast, the Savior said, "I am the good shepherd, . . . and I lay down my life for the sheep" (John 10:12–15). Many people today marry as hirelings. And when the wolf comes, they flee. This idea is wrong. It curses the earth, turning parents' hearts away from their children and from each other (see D&C 2).[39]

What a comfort it is to know that God himself is a part of our marriage. Paul wrote to the Romans, "If God be for us, who can be against us?" (Romans 8:31). We like to apply this verse to our marriage as well. And surely, God is for us. He wants our marriage to succeed. He wants *your* marriage to succeed. And the greatest tool we could possibly have in this effort is the gospel of Jesus Christ. In fact, everything we have in the gospel, *everything*—is to help us make and keep our marriage covenant. Is that a bold statement? It is, but I'm just repeating Elder Bruce R. McConkie:

> From the moment of birth into mortality to the time we are married in the temple, *everything we have in the whole gospel system* is to prepare and qualify us to enter that holy order of matrimony which makes us husband and wife in this life and in the world to come.
>
> Then from the moment we are sealed together by the power and authority of the holy priesthood—the power to bind on earth and have it sealed eternally in the heavens— from that moment *everything connected with revealed religion* is designed to help us keep the terms and conditions of our marriage covenant, so that this covenant will have efficacy, virtue, and force in the life to come.

Thus celestial marriage is the crowning ordinance of the gospel, the crowning ordinance of the house of the Lord. Thus the family unit is the most important organization in time or in eternity.[40]

What a blessing it is to know that I have the kingdom of God on earth behind me to help me in my marriage, and so do you. Don't forget to remember the covenant that you've made with God, and that he has made with you and your spouse!

If We Had Another Q & A Today

After several years of marriage, my sister-in-law, Tiffany, was often saddened by the conversations that took place at get-togethers (such as her book club meetings) with other women. It seemed inevitable that the discussion would decay into a gripe session about husbands, even when the comments began innocently enough.

In an attempt to create an evening where marriage and husbands were celebrated, Tiffany organized a neighborhood event to "celebrate marriage," complete with invitations, activities, and refreshments. Her girlfriends were invited to share some of their favorite ideas for creating romance and strengthening their marriages—creative dates and fun getaways—and share them with each other in her home. Tiffany took the initiative and completely turned things around. Can you imagine what a different world we would have if every neighborhood had a Tiffany? Or if every neighborhood held a regular "celebrate marriage" event?

Was Tiffany on some kind of community council? No. She held no official position. It's worthy of note, however, that she is a member of the largest women's organization in the world—the Relief Society—where women stand as witnesses of God at all times, in all things, in all places, and in all neighborhoods. Sister Sheri Dew taught:

We are here to *influence* the world rather than be influenced *by* the world. If we could unleash the *full* influence of covenant-keeping women, the kingdom of God would change overnight.

*"Satan's greatest threat today
is to destroy the family, and to
make a mockery of the law
of chastity and the sanctity of
the marriage covenant."*

—*President Harold B. Lee*[41]

No one has more influence on husbands than wives, on children than their mothers, or on young men than young women. Show me the women of *any* family or community, and I will show you the character and soul of that family and community. I repeat, if we would unleash the *full* influence of covenant-keeping women, the kingdom of God would change overnight.[42]

Tiffany would describe herself as a normal mother of five. But Tiffany is anything but normal. She is a covenant-keeping woman who caught the "celebrate marriage" spirit. Then she "unleashed" a bit of her righteous influence on the neighborhood, and changed a little bit of the world.

Of course it is a righteous desire to want your husband to be the man he ought to be. But "step one" in that process is to get the Spirit of the Lord into your marriage, and that may require some soul-searching, some change, and perhaps even some repentance on the part of both husband and wife.

So, let's say that question we started with were to come up again at another Q & A. Hopefully, there would be someone better qualified to answer the question than I am. But because of that sister in Cincinnati, I think I'd be much better prepared to respond this time, although it's a question that deserves more time than a sixty-second answer. So, to summarize this little book, here's what I'd say if I got that question today . . . it's not much, but it's the best I've got:

That's a tough question. You've probably already learned that nagging doesn't work, and criticism doesn't work either. What you're really asking for is a change of heart for someone else. And as they say, the only person who really *wants* to be changed is a baby with a messy diaper. The agent of change throughout the scriptures is the Holy Ghost. This means you have to invite the Spirit into your marriage in as many ways as possible. This also means you've got to kick the adversary out. Stop criticizing, stop complaining, stop resenting, start forgiving, start loving. The greater the presence of the Spirit in your home, the more it will work on his heart and the better the chance for change.

Make your focus not just on improving him, but on improving the marriage. In a healthy marriage, you'll have an easier time talking about these kinds of things. In the meantime, clarify your expectations. Make sure he knows what you want. Maybe he never had family home evening in his home, or maybe he doesn't know what priesthood leadership looks like. Maybe he's tried it before, and he failed and felt stupid. Men don't like to feel stupid, and they'll go to great lengths not to let it happen again. You may have other clues as to why certain things are not happening in your home. You know more about his past than any of us—once you know exactly why, you'll be in a better position to help.

Also, ask for things in smaller bites. Instead of asking him to be the patriarch in the family for the rest of eternity, tell him what you need that night. "Honey, I need you to call the kids together at 7:00 P.M., then I need you to make some comments after the lesson at about 7:45, then ask someone to pray."

Anytime he shows that leadership you're looking for, be very generous and specific in your praise and appreciation. The more he feels respected and admired, the more his best traits will come out. Also, the more you act in kind and loving ways, the more he will respond in the same way. Read his patriarchal blessing, and make the effort to treat him as if he is the priesthood leader you want him to be, and the chances are better that he'll rise to your expectations.

In the meantime, never give up. You have a covenant marriage. God is a partner in your marriage. He loves you both, and he wants you to succeed.

That's the best I've got. I sincerely hope it was helpful. I've seen difficult marriages, and I've seen divorces in my own extended family, which increased my desire to find a way to help this woman in Cincinnati find some answers.

I love being married. I am a big fan of my marriage, but I'm also a big fan of marriage in general. I think marriage makes us all better people and blesses our whole society. Most importantly, I hope that the Lord will bless your marriage with the presence of the Holy Ghost. I can think of no greater blessing.

As a husband of thirteen years, I am thankful beyond words for my wife, for her respect and encouragement for me even when I fall short. If it's really true that "behind every good man is a good woman," then I know I've got it made.

Notes

1. "Know This, That Every Soul Is Free," in *Hymns of The Church of Jesus Christ of Latter-day Saints* (Salt Lake City: The Church of Jesus Christ of Latter-day Saints, 1985), no. 240.
2. John L. Lund, *The Art of Giving and Receiving Criticism* (Salt Lake City: The Communications Company, 1997), 184.
3. Ibid., 19.
4. H. Burke Peterson, "Remember the Simple Things," in Douglas E. Brinley and Daniel K Judd, eds., *Eternal Companions* (Salt Lake City: Bookcraft, 1995), 4; emphasis in original.
5. Ibid.
6. Patricia Love and Steven Stosny, *How to Improve Your Marriage Without Talking About It* (New York: Broadway Books, 2007), 66–68.

7. Virginia H. Pearce, *A Heart Like His* (Salt Lake City: Deseret Book, 2006), 40; emphasis in original.

8. See C. Max Caldwell, "Love of Christ," *Ensign,* November 1992, 29.

9. Douglas E. Brinley, "The Keys of Marital Success—Part 1," in Brinley and Judd, *Eternal Companions,* 80.

10. *The Writings of Camilla Eyring Kimball,* edited by Edward L. Kimball (Salt Lake City: Deseret Book, 1988), 114.

11. Hugh W. Pinnock, "Ten Keys to Successful Dating and Marriage Relationships," in *Brigham Young University 1981 Fireside and Devotional Speeches* (Provo, Utah: Brigham Young University, 1981), 71.

12. Joni Hilton, "Equal Opportunity Disillusionment," http://www.meridianmagazine.com/circleofsisters/051031equal.html

13. Stephen R. Covey and Truman G. Madsen, *Marriage and Family: Gospel Insights* (Salt Lake City: Bookcraft, 1983), 154.

14. Cory H. Maxwell, ed., *The Neal A. Maxwell Quote Book* (Salt Lake City: Bookcraft, 1997), 206.

15. John L. Lund, *For All Eternity* (American Fork, Utah: Covenant Communications, 2008), 46–47.

16. Ibid., 13.

17. Deborah Tannen, *You Just Don't Understand* (New York: Ballantine Publishers, 1990), 81.

18. Lund, *For All Eternity,* 41.

19. Barbara and Allan Pease, *Why Men Don't Listen and Women Can't Read Maps* (New York: Welcome Rain Publishers, 2000), 96.

20. Love and Stosny, *How to Improve Your Marriage without Talking About It,* 71.

21. Wendy Watson, *Purity and Passion* (Salt Lake City: Bookcraft, 2001), 32.

22. Joseph L. Townsend, "Let Us Oft Speak Kind Words," in *Hymns,* no. 232.

23. As quoted in John-Roger and Peter McWilliams, *Do It! Let's Get Off Our Buts* (Los Angeles, CA: Prelude Press, 1991), 172.

24. Brent A. Barlow, *What Husbands Expect of Wives* (Salt Lake City: Deseret Book, 1983), 1.

25. E. E. LeMasters, *Parents in Modern America,* cited in Barlow, *What Husbands Expect of Wives,* 32; emphasis added.

26. Quoted in Laura Schlessinger, *The Proper Care and Feeding of Husbands* (New York: HarperCollins, 2004), 47–48.

27. H. Burke Peterson, "Unrighteous Dominion," *Ensign,* July 1989, 10.

28. Polly Block, in Joni Hilton, "Being Unequally Yoked," http://www.meridianmagazine.com/circleofsisters/051024 yoked.html

29. Joe J. Christensen, *One Step at a Time* (Salt Lake City: Deseret Book, 1996), 21.

30. Ezra Taft Benson, "Beware of Pride," *Ensign,* May 1989, 5.

31. Marjorie Pay Hinckley, *Small and Simple Things* (Salt Lake City: Deseret Book 2003), 31.

32. See Gary Chapman, *The Five Love Languages* (Chicago: Northfield Publishers, 1995).

33. Charles B. Beckert, *What Husbands Wish Wives Knew about Men* (American Fork: Covenant Recordings, 1983), audiocassette, side two.

34. Beverly Campbell, *You Don't Need to Slay My Dragons,*

Just Take Out the Trash (Salt Lake City: Deseret Book, 2008), 136–37.

35. Goethe, quoted in Stephen R. Covey, *How to Succeed with People* (Salt Lake City: Deseret Book, 1971), 43.

36. Merrilee Browne Boyack, *Strangling Your Husband Is NOT an Option* (Salt Lake City: Deseret Book, 2006), 124–25; emphasis in original.

37. Ezra Taft Benson, "To the 'Youth of the Noble Birthright,'" *Ensign,* May 1986, 43.

38. Elaine Jack, "Identity of a Young Woman," *Ensign,* November 1989, 87.

39. Bruce C. Hafen, "Covenant Marriage," *Ensign,* November 1996, 26.

40. Bruce R. McConkie, "Salvation Is a Family Affair," *Improvement Era,* June 1970, 43; emphasis added.

41. Harold B. Lee, *The Teachings of Harold B. Lee,* edited by Clyde J. Williams (Salt Lake City: Bookcraft, 1996), 227.

42. Sheri Dew, "Awake, Arise, and Come unto Christ," in *Awake, Arise, and Come unto Christ: Talks from the 2008 BYU Women's Conference* (Salt Lake City: Deseret Book, 2009), 13.

Index

INDEX